AF260836

Published by UTU Media® - © 2026 Bridget Irby

ISBN - 9781966130024
Unless indicated otherwise, all Scriptures marked KJV are taken from the KING JAMES VERSION (KJV): KING JAMES VERSION, public domain.
Printed in the United States of America

Dear Reader,
This Book Is Dedicated To You.

Your journey may not always be easy but, it is worth it.
I pray you find the words inside helpful and healing.

Dear Friend,

Fear has a way of taking up space it doesn't deserve.
It disguises itself as caution, wisdom, logic, preparation, or "being realistic."
It convinces us that staying on the sidelines is safer than stepping onto the battlefield.

But fear is not wisdom.
Fear is not protection.
Fear is not the voice of God.

Fear is a spiritual attack designed to immobilize God's people — and it's been working for far too long.

Just like Israel's army in the valley facing Goliath, many of God's daughters are standing still, discussing strategy, rehearsing the risk, negotiating with their insecurities, and calling it "being responsible." Meanwhile, the enemy is shouting threats from the field, hoping you stay exactly where you are: quiet, hesitant, and spiritually frozen.

But here's the truth:
You are not called to be afraid.
You are called to be a warrior.

Fear stops you.
Courage moves you.
Fear shrinks your life.
Faith expands it.
Fear steals your calling.
Courage activates it.

God didn't build you to hide.
He built you to fight — in His strength, with His authority, under His covering.

This study is going to confront fear gently, honestly, and powerfully. Not with shame or condemnation, but with truth and courage. You will see how fear has operated in your life… and you will learn how to break its influence forever.

By the time you finish these eight weeks, you will not be a woman consulting your fears.
You will be a woman walking in your calling.

Fear may come knocking — but you will not answer it anymore.

This is your moment.
Your battlefield.
Your breakthrough.
Your David anointing.

God is calling you out of hiding and into holy courage.

Let's step onto the field together,

Bridget

xoxo

Christian Friends Are The Best Friends!

There are moments in life when loneliness feels like it's closing in from every direction. Not the quiet kind of alone that brings rest, but the heavy kind that settles into your chest and makes everything feel harder — breathing, thinking, hoping. Sometimes loneliness shows up after heartbreak. Sometimes after disappointment. Sometimes after transition. And sometimes, it just appears, even when you're surrounded by people.

I've lived in that kind of loneliness. I've sat in rooms full of noise and still felt unseen. I've been in seasons where I didn't know who to trust, where to lean, or how to ask for help. And if you're holding this book, I want you to hear this with gentleness and truth:

Loneliness is not who you are.
 It is not your identity.
 It is not your forever.
 And it is not a sign that something is wrong with you.

You were created for connection — deep, safe, God-centered connection. But life has a way of pulling us away from what we were made for. Hurt hardens us. Disappointment distances us. Fear isolates us. And slowly, loneliness becomes the air we breathe.

But not anymore.

This study is your invitation back into the life God designed for you — one where you are surrounded, supported, strengthened, and known. You will uproot lies, break unhealthy patterns, rebuild trust, and open your heart again. You'll learn to connect — not from fear or striving, but from identity and wholeness.

I pray that as you walk through these pages, you feel God sitting with you... speaking to you... guiding you back into the community He has prepared for you.

You are not called to be alone.
 You are called to belong.

Let's rebuild together.

Lots of Love,

Bridget

xoxo

Hey Friend,

Fear stole years from me. Years of overthinking. Years of hesitation. Years where I felt called but didn't feel capable. Fear told me I wasn't ready, wasn't strong enough, wasn't spiritual enough, wasn't safe.

And for a long time... I believed it.

This study was born out of my own journey of breaking fear — not once, but over and over again, until courage became my new normal. God didn't shame me for being afraid. He invited me deeper. He strengthened me. He taught me how to fight.

I wrote this study for every woman who feels stuck...
every woman who wants to be bold but feels held back...
every woman who senses God nudging her but can't seem to move...
every woman who has a calling but is terrified to step into it.

If fear has been hovering over your life, your decisions, your relationships, or your future... you are in the right place.

These pages will challenge you.
They will stretch you.
But they will also free you.

As you read, I pray you hear God whisper:
"Daughter, you were born for this."

May this study ignite your courage, silence fear, awaken your faith, and prepare you for the battles you are anointed to win.

Let's fight together — and win.

Love you,
Bridget

Hey there, superstar!

I'm so proud of you for starting this journey and because I'm not about to send you out there empty-handed, I've got some awesome resources to help you on your journey.

Think of these as your toolkit. They're like the Swiss Army knife of emotional and spiritual growth - versatile, handy, and they might just save you in a pinch (though maybe don't try to use them to open a can or cut down a small tree).

To access the resources, simply create your free account at www.youarenotcalled.com.

Inside, you'll have to the above resources plus much more!

A Not-So-Boring-But-

Very-Important

Disclaimer

(Please Read This, Even If You

Usually Skip These Things)

Before we dive into this adventure together, we need to have a little chat. You know, the kind that usually comes with a cup of coffee and a "Now, don't freak out, but..." opener. So, grab your beverage of choice (I won't judge if it's not coffee), and let's get real for a moment.

First things first: I am not a doctor, therapist, counselor, or any other type of licensed mental health professional. I know, shocking right? Despite my incredible ability to dispense wisdom and wit (if I do say so myself), my qualifications are more in the realm of "life experience" and "passionate Jesus follower" than "Ph.D. in Psychology."

This book, as awesome as it is (and trust me, it's pretty awesome), is not meant to replace the invaluable work of trained professionals. Think of it more as a heart-to-heart with a friend who's been there, done that, and got the t-shirt (and maybe a few therapy sessions) to prove it.

If you're dealing with severe anger issues, depression, anxiety, or any other mental health concerns, **please, please, PLEASE seek help from a qualified professional.** They have tools in their toolbox that go way beyond what I can offer here. *(Plus, they probably have comfier couches for you to sit on while you talk.)*

This book is meant to be a companion on your journey, not your only guide. It's like having a workout buddy – super helpful and motivating, but not a substitute for a trained physical therapist if you've got a serious injury.

So, if at any point while reading this book you think, "Wow, I could really use some professional help with this," then congratulations! You've just had an incredibly mature and self-aware moment. Seriously, give yourself a pat on the back, then go find yourself a therapist. Your future self will thank you.

Remember, seeking help is not a sign of weakness. It's a sign that you're brave enough to admit you don't have all the answers (welcome to the club, by the way) and smart enough to ask for guidance. That's the kind of wisdom that would make Solomon proud!

Now, with all that said, I truly believe that this book has the potential to be a powerful tool in your spiritual and emotional growth journey. Just think of it as one piece of your "becoming-the-best-version-of-yourself" puzzle, not the whole picture.

So, are we clear? This book = awesome friend and spiritual cheerleader. Trained professionals = necessary allies for serious stuff. You = amazing child of God who deserves all the help and support you can get.

Alright, now that we've got that out of the way, let's get back to the good stuff. You've got a life-changing journey ahead of you, and I, for one, can't wait to see where it takes you. Just remember, if the road gets too bumpy, don't be afraid to call in some professional reinforcements. After all, even Batman needed Alfred, right?

Remember…

There's no rush.

You and me, love, we've got our whole lives to figure this thing out. Don't let rushing steal your joy.

There's no wrong answer.

This is unique to you and you simply cannot get it wrong. Just be honest with yourself and we can go from there.

You are doing great.

High five sister! Just the fact that you are here, with God, working on you says everything. Congratulations!

Week One

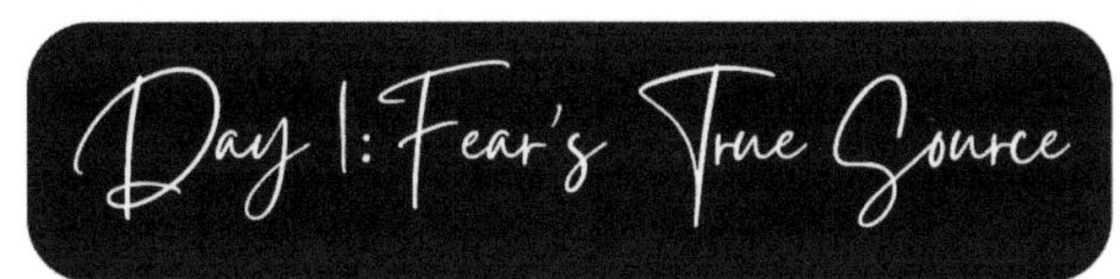

Fear feels emotional, but its origin is spiritual, which is why it feels so powerful and so destructive. It doesn't come from your personality, your past, your "overthinking tendencies," or anything rooted in logic or wisdom. Scripture is clear: fear is a spirit — a strategic, targeted attack from the enemy meant to immobilize you. When Paul wrote 2 Timothy 1:7, he wasn't being poetic; he was giving you a diagnosis. If fear didn't come from God, then you don't have to keep it, manage it, submit to it, obey it, or live under it. Fear is not your inheritance, your identity, your "thorn in the flesh," or your personality type. It is a weapon, and it is aimed directly at the parts of you the enemy fears most.

Fear attacks your calling, your confidence, your courage, your voice, your obedience, your relationships, and your decisions. It doesn't show up randomly — it shows up in the areas where you are most anointed. If the enemy can make you afraid of the very thing God called you to do, he never has to fight you directly; you'll retreat on your own. This is why fear feels suffocating, overwhelming, and convincing. Fear is a spiritual assault designed to push you backward while God is calling you forward.

And here is the truth fear never wants you to discover: you don't beat fear by becoming stronger; you beat fear by recognizing that it is not from God and refusing to agree with it. The moment you stop agreeing with fear, its power begins to break. Fear loses influence the second you expose it. Today is about dragging fear out of the shadows, refusing to let it operate undercover, and recognizing that what has been calling the shots in your life was never God's voice. Fear has been directing your steps long enough. You are not meant to live controlled by a spirit God never gave you.

Today, we expose fear at the root. We shine light on every tactic it has used to intimidate you. We refuse partnership with its lies. You are stepping into a new way of seeing fear — not as something permanent, not as something personal, but as something spiritual that can be resisted. Fear does not get to define your reactions, decisions, dreams, or calling. It's time to take back the territory.

Bible Reading

READ 2 TIMOTHY 1:7 (KJV)

Journal Prompt:

Where has fear shown up in your life recently?

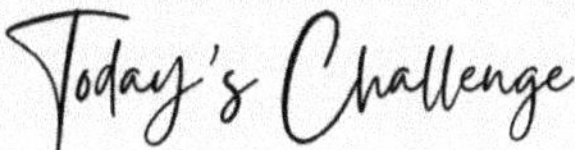

Today's Challenge

Today, identify one fear in your life and declare aloud:
"Fear, you are not from God. You do not belong to me."
Say it out loud.
Say it with authority.

Fear rarely walks through the front door. It doesn't usually crash into your life loudly or dramatically. Instead, it sneaks in quietly, subtly, slowly, slipping through cracks you didn't even realize were open. Fear often begins forming long before you ever recognize it, weaving itself into moments that seemed small at the time. It enters through experiences that shake your sense of safety. Trauma can open the door instantly, when something unexpected or painful happens and your nervous system declares, "We're not safe anymore." Your body remembers what you survived, and fear begins building its case around that moment.

Fear also enters through disappointment. When something you prayed for falls apart, or when life doesn't unfold the way you believed it would, your heart starts protecting itself by assuming the worst. You begin rehearsing negative outcomes as a way to avoid being hurt again. The enemy loves to use disappointment because it quietly shifts your expectations from hope to fear without you noticing. And when uncertainty shows up — when you're stepping into something new, stretching into unfamiliar territory, or walking in obedience without knowing the outcome — fear whispers the same tired questions: "What if you fail? What if you fall? What if everything collapses?" The unknown becomes the perfect breeding ground for fear.

Fear can enter through the words of others, especially authority figures, parents, mentors, or voices from your past who shaped your view of yourself. Sometimes the fear you're fighting isn't even yours — it's someone else's fear that you adopted as truth. And fear also enters through spiritual warfare, because the enemy studies you carefully. He sees your patterns, your vulnerabilities, your hopes, and your wounds. He knows exactly where to aim to create doubt, insecurity, or hesitation.

But the most common doorway fear uses is lack of identity. When you don't fully know who you are in Christ, fear tries to define you. When you don't know what God has spoken over you, fear fills the silence. When you don't understand the authority you carry, fear feels bigger and louder than it truly is. Experiences may open the door, but fear grows through agreement. It gains strength when you start believing its messages.
Today isn't about shaming yourself for the doors fear used; it's about identifying them so you can close them. Fear may have gotten in somehow — but it doesn't get to stay.

Bible Reading

Journal Prompt:

Which experiences opened the door for fear in your life?

Fear doesn't just impact your emotions — it impacts your entire life. It shapes decisions, relationships, expectations, and the way you see yourself. Fear costs you far more than you realize because it slowly convinces you that safety is the highest goal. It steals opportunities because anything that feels uncertain automatically feels unsafe. You start avoiding risks, open doors, or God-given assignments simply because you can't predict the outcome. Fear steals relationships because vulnerability becomes terrifying. It becomes easier to stay guarded, distant, or emotionally unavailable than to risk being seen or hurt. Fear steals joy because you're always bracing for impact, waiting for something to go wrong, assuming goodness won't last.

Fear steals obedience because faith always requires movement. God rarely gives you step-by-step clarity, so fear uses the unknown as leverage to keep you still. It steals calling by convincing you that someone else would be better, stronger, more prepared, or more capable. Fear doesn't need you to reject God to win; it simply needs you to hesitate. And hesitation, over time, kills destiny. The enemy doesn't have to derail your purpose through rebellion — he just needs to keep you frozen long enough that you start believing the opportunity "wasn't God" and walk away from what was meant for you.

Fear doesn't just paralyze you — it shrinks your world. You start living small, thinking small, expecting small, praying small, deciding small, and showing up small. You survive, but you do not flourish. You make it through the day, but you never step into the fullness of who God created you to be. And perhaps the most heartbreaking cost of fear is how many of God's daughters have been convinced that playing safe is holy. But nowhere in Scripture does God bless fear-led caution. He blesses courage. He blesses obedience. He blesses action. He blesses movement. He blesses faith.

Today, God is inviting you to recognize the true cost of living afraid — not to shame you, but to free you. When you see what fear has stolen, you can finally decide to stop letting it take anything else. Fear has taken enough. It doesn't get another day.

Bible Reading

READ PROVERBS 28:1 (KJV)

Journal Prompt:

What has fear cost you emotionally?

Write a short list titled:
"What Fear Has Stolen From Me."
Then circle one thing you want back.

Fear almost never announces itself honestly. It rarely says, "I'm fear." Instead, it whispers things that sound reasonable, careful, even responsible. It says, "I'm just being wise." "I'm being realistic." "I'm protecting myself." "I need more information." "I want to be careful." Fear is clever. It dresses itself up as logic, maturity, caution, and common sense, which is why it becomes so easy to mistake fear for discernment. Fear sounds thoughtful, but its goal is to keep you still.

Israel's army made the same mistake. When Goliath roared across the valley, they didn't fall on the ground declaring, "We're terrified!" They started strategizing, discussing, analyzing, weighing outcomes, and calculating risks. What they called wisdom was actually fear wearing armor. It looked wise. It sounded reasonable. It felt justified. But it was still fear. And here's the truth: fear loves to masquerade as wisdom so you won't rebuke it. If fear can convince you it's protecting you, you'll never question its influence.

Fear pretends it's helping you avoid danger — but what it's really helping you avoid is destiny. It will justify passivity by calling it patience. It will rationalize disobedience by calling it discernment. It will spiritualize hesitation by calling it caution. Fear will convince you that waiting is holy, especially when the thing God asked you to do feels costly or uncertain. But fear isn't keeping you safe — it's keeping you stuck.

David responded differently. He didn't outthink Goliath. He didn't gather more information, consult more opinions, or overanalyze the risk. He didn't sit in a holy huddle trying to calculate the safest option. He ran toward the giant. Not because he was reckless, careless, or naïve — but because he was convinced of God. His confidence wasn't in his slingshot; it was in God's authority. David knew that real wisdom aligns with God's voice, not your comfort.

Real wisdom moves in obedience, not endless overthinking. Real wisdom trusts God more than it trusts fear. Real wisdom steps forward even when your feelings tell you to retreat. Today, God is inviting you to examine the places in your life where fear has dressed itself up as wisdom. Not to shame you — but to free you from a counterfeit version of discernment that has quietly held you back. Fear may sound wise, but wisdom rooted in God will always lead you forward.

Bible Reading

READ PROVERBS 3:5 (KJV)

Journal Prompt:
Where has fear disguised itself as wisdom in your life?

Today's Challenge

Write one place where you've allowed fear to pretend it was wisdom.
Then ask God:
"Is this You, or is this fear?"

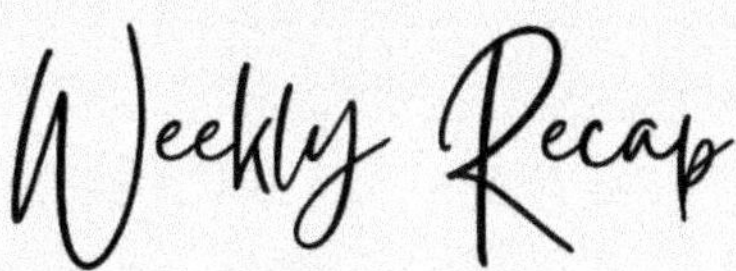

Weekly Recap

This week, you learned the truth about fear — not the surface-level truth you've heard a hundred times, but the deep spiritual reality fear never wanted you to understand. You discovered that fear is a spirit, not a personality trait, and that it enters quietly through wounds, disappointments, and lies you didn't always recognize. You also saw how fear costs you more than you realized, and how it often disguises itself as wisdom so you won't confront it or call it what it truly is.

Fear's power thrives in the dark. It grows stronger when it operates unnoticed, unchallenged, and unexposed. But once it's exposed, it begins to crumble. This week wasn't about eliminating every fearful feeling — it was about recognizing fear's voice, its tactics, and its strategy so you can refuse agreement. When you see fear clearly, you stop obeying it. When you understand its source, you stop trusting it. When you recognize how it entered, you break its access. And when you acknowledge what it has stolen, you reclaim your ground and begin taking back what fear has tried to own.

You are already changing. Your awareness is changing. Your posture is changing. Your courage is rising in places that used to collapse under pressure. You are beginning to see when fear is talking, when fear is disguising itself, and when fear is trying to lead. What once felt normal now feels exposed, and what once felt powerful now feels smaller in the light of truth.

Next week, you will discover God's response to your fear — the truth, comfort, and strength He provides for every battle you face. Freedom begins with exposure, and you've already started walking out of fear. You are not the same person who began this week, and the shift happening inside you is only the beginning of the freedom God is leading you into.

Father,

Thank you for exposing fear in my life.

Thank You for revealing its tactics, its lies, and its influence.

Strengthen my heart, renew my mind, and break every agreement fear has made with my past, my identity, or my decisions.

Fill me with courage for the battles ahead.

Lead me into boldness, confidence, and truth.

I choose freedom, Lord — and I choose You.

In Jesus' name,
Amen.

Week Two

Day 1: God Doesn't Shame You For Fear

Fear often brings shame with it. We think, "I should be stronger," "I should be more spiritual," "I shouldn't feel like this," or "I should trust God more." But God never shames His children for feeling afraid. Not once in Scripture does He say, "How dare you feel fear." Instead, He says, "I am with you," "I will help you," "Do not be afraid," and "Take courage — I am here." God's response to fear is not condemnation; it's compassion.

Think about every moment in Scripture where someone was afraid: Moses trembling before Pharaoh, Joshua stepping into leadership after Moses died, Gideon hiding in the winepress, Mary facing an impossible calling, the disciples in the storm. God didn't rebuke their fear; He reassured them. Fear is a human signal, not a spiritual failure.

But here's the difference between staying afraid and becoming fearless: fear becomes bondage when you agree with it, but fear becomes breakthrough when you bring it to God. God meets fear with presence, strength, identity, truth, and power. Fear says, "You're alone." God says, "I am with you." Fear says, "You're not enough." God says, "I am your strength." Fear says, "This will destroy you." God says, "I will uphold you." Fear says, "You can't handle this." God says, "I will help you."

His response is always tender, but also transformative. He doesn't scold, shame, or demand perfection; He meets you where you are. Fear signals that God wants you to rely on Him, not on your own strength. It's an invitation to intimacy, not a condemnation for weakness.

Today, instead of hiding from God because you're afraid, bring your fear straight to Him. Speak it out. Name it. Lay it at His feet. He's not disappointed in you; He's ready to deliver you. He's already present, already strong, and already capable of carrying you through whatever feels impossible. Your fear is not a failure — it's a doorway to God's power and presence, if you let Him meet you there.

Bible Reading

Journal Prompt:

What do you believe God thinks about

your fear?

Today's Challenge

Write a fear you've been hiding from God.
Then pray:
"Here it is, Lord. Meet me in this."

Day 2 – God Fights Your Battles With You

Fear feels overwhelming because you assume you're fighting alone. It feels like the weight is on you: your strength, your wisdom, your capability, your preparation, your plan. But God never intended you to fight fear—or anything else—alone. He is not a distant commander shouting instructions from heaven. He is Emmanuel: God with us, God beside you, God within you.

When Israel stood paralyzed in front of Goliath, God wasn't waiting for someone strong enough. He was waiting for someone willing enough. David knew something the others didn't: the battle wasn't his; it was God's. Fear shrinks when you shift from "I must overcome this" to "God and I will overcome this together."

God doesn't throw you into the battlefield and hope you survive. He steps onto the field with you. Fear wants you isolated; God wants you empowered. Fear wants you overwhelmed; God wants you confident. Fear wants you hesitant; God wants you moving forward. You are not alone in your calling, your healing, your battles, your obedience, or your decisions.

The presence of God is your courage. The power of God is your strength. The voice of God is your direction. The protection of God is your covering. He is not passive or distant—He is actively present in the moments where fear threatens to paralyze you. God fights the battles you cannot, covers the areas you feel weak, and strengthens the places you feel vulnerable. Fear may try to convince you otherwise, but God's truth is louder: you are never alone.

Today, let this settle in your spirit: you are never, ever fighting alone. When fear rises, remember you are partnered with the Almighty. When obstacles appear insurmountable, remember your battles belong to Him. When doubt whispers that you can't, remember His presence, His power, His voice, and His protection are already with you. This truth transforms fear into courage, hesitation into action, and isolation into companionship. You are not walking this journey alone—God is fighting every battle alongside you.

Bible Reading

Journal Prompt:

Where have you been trying to fight

alone?

Today's Challenge

Write the hardest battle you're facing right now.
Then declare:
"Lord, this battle is Yours."

When God prepares you to overcome fear, He doesn't start with your situation. He starts with your identity. Before Gideon ever fought a battle, God called him "Mighty warrior." Before Joshua stepped into leadership, God told him, "Be strong and courageous — I am with you." Before Mary carried the Savior, the angel greeted her, "Highly favored." Before David faced Goliath, he was already anointed king. Identity comes first. Courage comes second. Breakthrough comes third.

Fear attacks who you think you are. God restores who He already knows you are. Fear says, "You're weak, you're fragile, you're unprepared, you're over your head." God says, "You're chosen, you're empowered, you're protected, you're anointed, you're called, you're mine." Fear screams limitations. God speaks identity. Every time fear rises, the real question is not, "Is the situation too big for me?" but, "Do I remember who I am?" Fear makes you forget. Identity makes you fearless.

When you know who God says you are, fear loses its grip. You stop shrinking, you stop hesitating, you stop apologizing for taking up space. You begin to walk in confidence, to speak with authority, and to move forward with courage. Identity is not just a concept — it is your spiritual armor, your spiritual authority, your spiritual anchor. It is what protects you, empowers you, and reminds you of the truth in moments when fear tries to cloud your mind.

Today, let God speak to who you are, not just what you face. Let Him remind you that you are chosen for this moment, equipped for the battles ahead, and anointed for the calling in front of you. Fear may rise, but it cannot redefine your identity. Fear may try to paralyze you, but it cannot undo what God has already spoken. Your power, your courage, your boldness, and your breakthrough all begin with remembering who you are in Him. Identity is the foundation. Fear is the intruder. Let God remind you that your identity has already won.

Bible Reading

Journal Prompt:

What identity labels has fear given you?

Today's Challenge

Choose one identity God has given you.
Write it at the top of a page.
Under it, list three ways you will walk in it this week.

You cannot always control when fear rises, but you can absolutely control whether fear stays. Fear cannot survive the presence of God. Think about the disciples in the storm. They were panicking, certain they would die. Jesus woke up, spoke peace, and the storm obeyed. The presence of Jesus shifted the atmosphere instantly.

Fear dissolves in the presence of God because His presence brings peace, clarity, reassurance, authority, and strength. Fear thrives in separation but shrivels in closeness. This is why the enemy fights your intimacy with God so hard. If he can distract you, overwhelm you, or exhaust you, fear gains ground. Your courage isn't found in perfect circumstances; your courage is found in His presence.

You don't need more confidence. You need more closeness. You don't need more certainty. You need more connections. You don't need more strategy. You need more surrender. God's presence is not a feeling — it's a reality. He is always near, always ready, always available. You don't have to manufacture courage on your own. You don't have to figure out all the answers. You don't have to push through fear by sheer willpower. You simply need to draw close to Him, to step into His presence and allow His nearness to overshadow the fear.

Fear loses its power when confronted with the nearness of God. It cannot stand in an atmosphere saturated with His peace, His authority, and His strength. Wherever you feel panic, uncertainty, or dread, you can choose to shift your focus from the threat to the One who is greater than the threat. Closeness with God is your defense, your weapon, and your refuge.

Today, you don't have to fix your fear, solve your circumstances, or eliminate every anxious thought. You just have to get close to Him. Let His presence saturate your heart and mind. Let His peace rise above the storm. Let His authority silence the lies fear whispers. Fear may appear, but it cannot remain where God is. Draw near, trust Him, and watch fear dissolve.

Bible Reading

Journal Prompt:

What happens to your fear when you get

close to God?

Today's Challenge

Take 7 minutes today and sit in silence with God.

Let Him speak.

Let Him settle you.

Let Him break the fear.

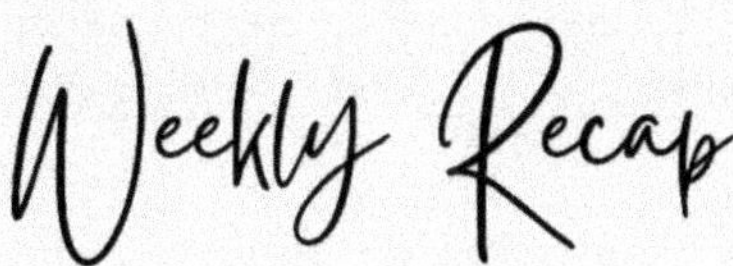

Weekly Recap

This week, you saw something powerful: God never responds to fear with shame — He responds with support. You learned that God meets your fear with compassion, fights your battles with you, speaks to your identity before your fear, and breaks fear with His presence. Fear tries to isolate you. It tries to convince you that you're the only one feeling this way. It tries to make you believe you must handle everything yourself.

But God steps in and says, "You are not alone. You are not unprotected. You are not unprepared. You are not weak." His response doesn't shame you. It reassures you, strengthens you, and calls you to trust Him. This week wasn't about trying to feel courageous; it was about learning to recognize God's nearness. You are not fighting fear by willpower. You are fighting fear through relationship.

As you move forward, you will begin to feel your spirit settle. Fear may still knock, but it won't control your steps. Fear may rise, but it will not rise above God's voice. You are becoming strong. You are becoming steady. You are becoming secure in His presence. His presence is your courage, His power is your strength, and His voice is your guidance.

Next week, we shift into the battlefield of the mind, learning how fear operates internally and how God gives you the tools to shut it down. You are learning to see fear for what it is, to confront it with God's truth, and to walk in freedom even when the enemy tries to whisper lies. Step into the days ahead knowing that fear no longer defines you — God's presence does.

Dear Father,

Thank You for walking with me through my fear.

Thank You for meeting me with compassion, identity, strength, and presence.

Help me continue to trust You deeply and lean on You completely.

Prepare my mind, my heart, and my spirit for the next level of freedom.

I choose courage.

I choose truth.

I choose You.

In Jesus' name,
Amen.

Week Three

Day 1: Fear Begins With A Thought

Fear doesn't begin with panic, or anxiety, or a racing heart, or spiraling emotions. Fear begins with a thought — a whisper, a possibility, a "what if," a scenario that doesn't even exist yet but suddenly feels real. Fear rarely shouts. It suggests: "What if this falls apart? What if they leave? What if you fail? What if you're wrong? What if God doesn't show up?" One subtle thought can trigger a full emotional storm.

But here's the truth fear doesn't want you to see: thoughts are not truth, thoughts are not prophecy, thoughts are not commands, thoughts are not identity, and thoughts are not destiny. Your mind is not a passive victim. Your mind is a spiritual battleground, and God has given you authority in it. 2 Corinthians 10:5 says to take every thought captive — not entertain it, not negotiate with it, not analyze it, not fear it. Take it, grab it, arrest it, evaluate it, replace it. Your thoughts are not in charge of you — you are in charge of them.

Fear's power is not in the thought itself, but in your agreement with it. When you accept fear's suggestion, it grows. When you refuse it, it dies. One small "yes" to fear can lead to hours of worry, hesitation, and avoidance, but one act of capturing a thought in God's authority can shift your whole day, your decisions, and your perspective.

Today, you begin reclaiming your mind. You begin to see thoughts as tools, not tyrants. You begin to recognize the whispers that masquerade as truth and learn to replace them with God's voice. You are learning that your mind is not a battlefield you lose — it is a space where God gives you victory.

Fear will continue to speak. But you have a choice: agreement or authority, surrender or capture, bondage or freedom. Every thought you take captive is a small victory, a step toward a fearless, obedient, Spirit-led life. Today is your day to begin seizing that authority and walking in mental freedom.

Journal Prompt:

What fearful thoughts show up most

often?

Today's Challenge

Write one recurring fearful thought.
Then write God's truth beside it.

Fear has a favorite strategy: it shows you a future that God never authored. Fear takes the unknown and fills it with worst-case scenarios, it takes possibilities and treats them like inevitabilities, it takes uncertainty and turns it into danger. Fear says, "You will lose everything, you will be rejected, you will fail, you will suffer, you will be alone, you will regret this." Fear is a storyteller, but it's a liar. Fear paints a future to paralyze your present.

But here's the truth: fear cannot see the future — it only predicts it based on your past. Fear studies your history, your patterns, your wounds, your disappointments. But fear has no revelation about your destiny. Fear can only project what has been, never what God is doing next. God speaks promise, fear speaks probability. God speaks destiny, fear speaks danger. God speaks breakthrough, fear speaks breakdown. Fear does not have authority to define what is coming, it only tries to define what could go wrong.

Every time you imagine the future with fear as your narrator, your courage dies. You hesitate, you shrink, you doubt, you stop pursuing God's calling and possibilities. But you are not powerless. Your imagination is a gift from God, a tool to dream, plan, and hope in alignment with His promises. Fear may attempt to hijack it, but you have the authority to reclaim it.

Today, you reclaim your imagination. You refuse to let fear be the storyteller of your life. You refuse to let worst-case scenarios dictate your decisions. You take the unknown and hand it back to God, letting Him define what is possible. You begin to envision the future with promise, hope, and destiny, not with probability, danger, and breakdown. You choose to align your thoughts about the future with God's voice, God's Word, and God's promises.

When you do this, fear loses its grip. Your mind becomes a place of possibility, faith, and courage. Your imagination becomes a battlefield for God's truth, not the enemy's lies. Today, take every fearful projection and replace it with God's vision. Your future belongs to Him, not fear.

Bible Reading

Journal Prompt:

What future scenarios has fear been
painting for you?

Today's Challenge

Write down one fearful future fear has shown you.
Then rewrite it with God's voice.

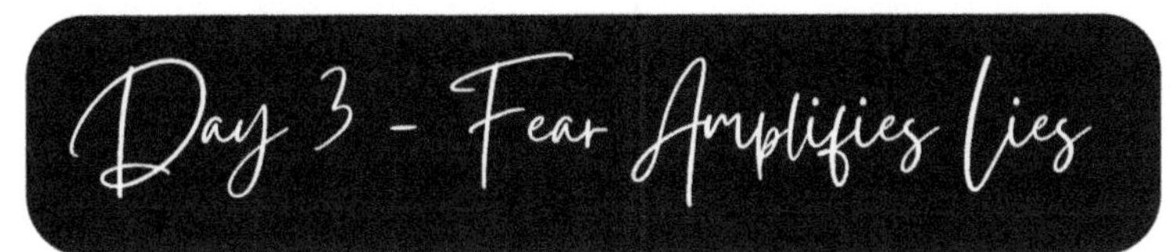

Fear doesn't start with a lie — it starts with an accusation: "You can't handle this, you're not good enough, you're not loved, you're not safe, you're going to fail." Then fear repeats it, echoes it, magnifies it, reinforces it. Fear doesn't need to be true, it just needs to be loud. And when fear says something long enough, it begins to feel familiar. And what feels familiar often feels true.

But here's the shift: lies don't become truth just because they become loud. God's truth never changes, your identity never changes, your calling never changes, God's protection never changes, God's promises never change. Fear's repetition does not equal revelation. The more fear speaks, the more you must speak back. You have authority to interrupt the pattern of lies. You don't need to negotiate with fear or wait for it to pass.

Jesus confronted lies with Scripture. He didn't debate them, he didn't rationalize them, he didn't emotionally process them — he declared truth. Fear is loud, but truth is louder. Fear is aggressive, but truth is authoritative. Fear is persistent, but truth is permanent. You can do the same. When fear begins to amplify lies, respond with the Word of God, with the promises He has spoken over your life, and with the reality of who you are in Christ.

Today, you stop letting fear's volume override God's voice. You refuse to let repeated accusations become your narrative. You declare what is true, not what feels true. You remind yourself of God's faithfulness, His protection, and His power in your life. You remind yourself that fear does not get the final say. The loudest voice in your mind is not fear — it is God.

When you choose to speak truth over fear, lies lose their grip. Your mind becomes a place of clarity, courage, and faith. Your spirit begins to trust God more than the whispers of fear. Today, declare the truth, and let it echo louder than fear ever could.

Bible Reading

**READ, REFLECT, & PRAY ON
JOHN 17:17 (KJV)**

Journal Prompt:

What lies has fear repeated to you?

Today's Challenge

Choose one lie fear has repeated.
Declare truth against it out loud.

Fear often feels automatic, instant, uncontrollable. A sound, a memory, a possibility — and suddenly your whole body reacts. But here's the freedom: fear can rise automatically, but you can interrupt it intentionally. Your first reaction is human, your second reaction is spiritual, and your second reaction is where your authority lives. Fear rises, but you choose whether it stays.

You interrupt fear by speaking Scripture, declaring your identity, taking thoughts captive, breathing in God's presence, calling on Jesus' name, moving your body, redirecting your focus, worshipping, rebuking the enemy, and choosing obedience. Fear is a pattern, and patterns can be broken. You can disrupt fear the moment it begins. You can stop fear before it spirals. You can shut down fear before it shapes your choices. Fear is fast, but the Spirit of God is faster. Fear is loud, but the authority of Jesus is louder. Fear is aggressive, but your identity is stronger.

You are not helpless. You are not fragile. You are not powerless in your thoughts. You are not at the mercy of your emotions. You have been given authority in Christ to respond, to intervene, and to act before fear dictates your behavior. Fear does not get the final say. Your obedience, your declaration, your faith, and your awareness of God's presence all work together to interrupt fear immediately.

Today, practice interrupting fear the moment it surfaces. Speak the truth of God's Word over your thoughts. Declare who you are in Christ. Take control of your focus and actions. Do not wait for fear to pass on its own. Instead, confront it, engage it, and stop it in its tracks.

Fear will rise — but you are stronger. Fear will speak — but your voice, anchored in Scripture and identity, is louder. Fear will try to control your mind, body, and spirit — but you have been equipped to respond, to reclaim, and to move forward with courage. In every moment, you have the power to interrupt fear — in seconds.

Bible Reading

Journal Prompt:

What does your first reaction to fear

usually look like?

Today's Challenge

Interrupt one fear today.
Speak truth.
Move your body.
Redirect your focus.
Change your atmosphere.

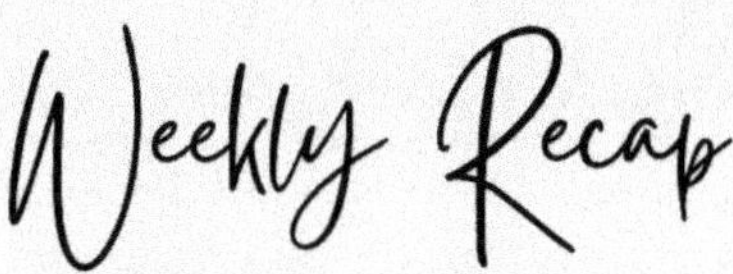

Weekly Recap

This week, you stepped onto the frontlines of your mind — the place where fear begins, grows, and takes root. And you learned how to stop it. You discovered that fear begins as a thought, shows false futures, repeats lies until they feel true, and can be interrupted immediately.

You are not a victim of fear. You are not at the mercy of your thoughts. You are not powerless against mental battles. Your mind is not a battlefield you're losing — it's a battlefield God is teaching you to win.

You are becoming more aware, more discerning, and more spiritually strong. You are learning to reject what is false and embrace what is true. You are learning to recognize fear instantly and interrupt it immediately. Fear no longer has the freedom to dictate your decisions, limit your courage, or shrink your vision.

This week didn't just expose fear — it empowered you. You're not only learning how fear works; you are learning how you work, how your spirit responds, how your thoughts move, and how your identity holds firm in the midst of mental attacks. Each step you take in awareness and action strengthens your mind and positions you to walk boldly into every circumstance God has prepared.

Next week, you will step into the David anointing — learning how to face giants, not coexist with them. You are prepared to move forward with clarity, courage, and confidence, armed with the spiritual tools to take every thought captive and to lead your mind rather than be led by fear. Your mental battlefield is becoming a place of victory.

Weekly Prayer

Dear Lord,

Thank You for renewing my mind this week.

Thank You for exposing fear's tactics and strengthening my spirit.

Teach me to take thoughts captive, interrupt fear quickly, and walk in the truth You speak over my life.

Prepare me for the courage and breakthrough ahead.

In Jesus' name,
Amen.

Week Four

Day 1: Giants Fall When You Being Afraid

Israel didn't lose to Goliath because they were weak. They lost because they were negotiating with fear. They stood on the sidelines analyzing how big he was, how loud he was, how strong he looked, and how risky the battle might be. Fear always invites you into conversation. It wants you to consider it, discuss it, respect it, accommodate it, and give it a seat at the table—long before it ever throws a punch.

David refused to negotiate. He didn't listen to Goliath. He didn't discuss strategy. He didn't wait for clarity. He didn't gather opinions. He didn't rehearse pros and cons or ask himself if he felt ready. David ran toward the giant because he understood something Israel hadn't realized: fear gains power every second you allow it to speak.

You cannot defeat what you keep negotiating with. You cannot conquer what you keep explaining away. You cannot get free from what you keep giving permission to influence your thoughts. Fear doesn't leave because you understand it or because you've finally analyzed the situation enough. Fear leaves because you confront it. It loses strength the moment you stop giving it an audience.

The Israelite soldiers thought their analysis was wisdom, but it was fear dressed up in logic. That's what fear does—it disguises itself as caution, overthinking, or being "realistic." It convinces you that waiting is wise, that more time will help, that more information will make you brave. But fear doesn't need clarity; it needs captivity. Fear wants more conversations, more what-ifs, more mental rehearsals of every possible failure.

But giant-killers understand this truth: you don't out-think fear, you out-obey God. Obedience breaks fear's influence because it shifts your focus from "What if I fail?" to "What did God say?" The giant wasn't defeated by a perfect plan; he was defeated by a willing heart.

Today, identify the places where you've been negotiating with fear—where you've been giving it time, attention, justification, or space to speak. Maybe it's a decision you keep delaying, a step you keep postponing, a conversation you keep avoiding, or a calling you keep doubting. Wherever you've been negotiating, stop the conversation. Shut down the debate. Fear's power ends where your obedience begins. And like David, you may discover that the giant was never as strong as the voice that tried to stop you from facing it.

Bible Reading

Journal Prompt:

Where have you been negotiating with fear?

Today's Challenge

Write down one place where fear has kept you on the sidelines.
Declare: "I'm done negotiating with fear."

David didn't become a giant-killer on the battlefield. He became a giant-killer in the field. While everyone else overlooked him, God was training him. The lion? Training. The bear? Training. The solitude? Training. The rejection from his family? Training. The small responsibilities? Training. Every unseen battle prepared him for a seen victory. Every moment, every challenge, every test in private was a rehearsal for the moment God called him to stand before a giant.

Fear tells you, "You're not ready. You're underqualified. You need more time. You need more experience." Fear wants you to compare your preparation to someone else's or to measure your courage against a standard you can't yet see. But God says, "I've already trained you. You're more prepared than you think." He meets you in the background, in the quiet, in the daily grind, in the moments nobody notices, and He builds what you need for the battles ahead. What seems ordinary or mundane is actually extraordinary preparation. What feels like waiting is actually building. What feels like struggle is actually strengthening.

The battles you fought in private—the struggles no one knows about, the victories that felt small, the valleys you survived—were all preparation. David didn't step onto the battlefield hoping God would show up. He stepped onto the battlefield remembering how God already had. He stepped with confidence rooted in experience and trust, not in fear or self-reliance.

You are not stepping into fear empty-handed. You are stepping in with history, with spiritual muscle memory, with evidence of God's faithfulness, and with weapons that have been tested. Nothing you've walked through was wasted. Every season has strengthened you for this one. Every tear, every trial, every moment of waiting has cultivated courage. Every small obedience has prepared you to act boldly when it matters most.

So today, when fear whispers, "You're not ready," remember your private victories. Remember the unseen moments where God trained your hands, sharpened your mind, and fortified your heart. You are more prepared than you think. God has been equipping you quietly, faithfully, and deliberately for the public victory that is coming. Stand ready. Step forward. Face the giant, not in your strength alone, but in the strength God has been building inside you all along.

Bible Reading

Journal Prompt:

What private battles has God used to strengthen you?

Today's Challenge
List three past victories God gave you.
Circle one you can lean on today for courage.

Day 3 – You Don't Need Their Armor

When David decided to face Goliath, Saul offered him his armor. It didn't fit. It wasn't made for him. It wasn't his assignment. The armor was heavy, cumbersome, and designed for someone else's battles, someone else's strengths, someone else's calling. David knew it wouldn't help him. He refused to carry someone else's strategy, someone else's expectations, someone else's version of safety. He understood a vital truth: what God calls you to do, He equips you to do — not someone else.

Fear often tries to convince you that you need someone else's tools, their experience, their qualifications, or their confidence to succeed. It whispers, "You're not ready. You're not strong enough. You need what they have." It wants you to compare, imitate, and rely on the familiar rather than trusting the gifts God has placed uniquely inside you. Fear points to someone else's armor, but faith points to your anointing. Fear measures by another person's standard; God measures by your calling.

Fear will try to make you think you need someone else's qualifications, personality, experience, methods, confidence, or calling to succeed. It will tell you that the only way to be safe, to be effective, or to win is to adopt someone else's approach. But God never anoints you to imitate someone else. He anoints you to walk in what He has placed inside you. Your courage doesn't come from someone else's armor; it comes from walking fully in your own anointing, in your own calling, in your own authority.

Faith calls you to trust God's provision, not someone else's plan. You were created for your story, your voice, your training, your identity, your gifts, and your authority. You don't need to wear someone else's armor. You need to embrace the armor God has given you. Every spiritual battle you face will be won not by imitating others but by stepping boldly into the gifts and anointing already in your hands.

Today, refuse the fear that wants to weigh you down with what doesn't fit. Step forward in your identity, your training, and your authority. The weapons God has given you are powerful, precise, and effective — if you choose to trust them and walk in them. You don't win battles using someone else's tools. You win by using the ones God has placed in your hands.

READ 1 SAM 17:39 (KJV)

Journal Prompt:

Where have you tried to wear someone else's "armor"?

Today's Challenge

Write one place where you've been carrying someone else's expectations.
Let it go today.

David didn't kill Goliath with new weapons. He didn't wait for a different season, a better tool, or a stronger platform. He killed him with what he already carried. A simple sling. A single stone. Skill he had developed in secret. Courage he had cultivated over time. Faith he had built through experience. Every quiet moment of preparation, every trial he faced in private, every small victory had equipped him for this defining battle.

Fear often tries to convince you that you're not ready, that you need more resources, more time, a bigger platform, a different season, or a stronger version of yourself. Fear whispers, "You need to be someone else, do something more, become more equipped before you can win." But God's voice is clear: "Use what's already in your hand." Your giant is not waiting on you to change into someone else — it's waiting on you to step forward in the gifts, abilities, and faith God has already placed within you.

The stone in David's hand represents what God has entrusted to you. It might be a testimony that encourages others. It might be a consistent prayer life that unlocks power in unseen ways. It might be a spiritual gift, a boldness, a promise, or a word God has spoken over your life. These are not small or incidental; these are divine tools, perfectly suited for your assignment. Fear wants you to underestimate them, to doubt them, or to ignore them. The enemy isn't afraid of your potential. He's afraid of your obedience.

Giants fall when you stop waiting to be more than you are and start using what you already are. Victory doesn't come from acquiring more; it comes from trusting what God has already given. Obedience activates your resources, unleashes your faith, and moves your courage into action. Every skill, every lesson, every spiritual breakthrough you've experienced has been preparing you to face your giant. You don't need a different weapon, a better season, or someone else's approval. You need to step forward in faith and take what's already in your hand.

Today, stop delaying. Stop waiting. Stop questioning your readiness. Your giant will not wait, but neither will your opportunity for victory. Use what God has already given you. Step forward with courage, faith, and obedience. Giants fall when you trust in the tools God has already placed in your hands.

READ 1 SAM 17:40 (KJV)

Journal Prompt:
What "stone" has God already placed in your hand?

Today's Challenge

Identify one "stone" God has given you — and use it today.

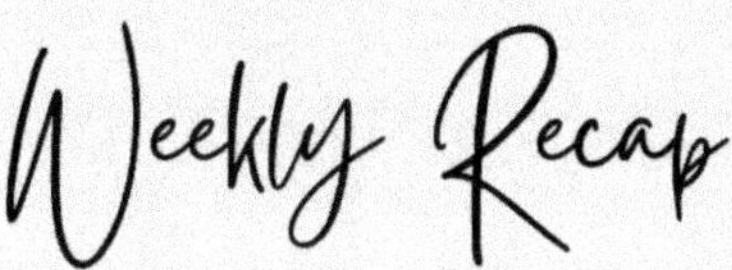

This week, something shifted in your spirit. Not a small, subtle shift — a warrior shift. A movement in your heart that changes how you see fear, your calling, and the battles in front of you. You discovered that giants fall when you stop negotiating with fear, that God has been training you in the secret place, that you don't need someone else's armor, and that victory comes when you use what God has already placed in your hands.

Fear wants you frozen on the sidelines, overanalyzing your next step, questioning your readiness, and explaining your hesitation. It whispers lies about inadequacy, lack, and delay. But giant-killers are different. They run toward the fight. They trust the preparation God has already done in their lives. They refuse to carry weapons or strategies that aren't theirs. They step forward with what God has given them, confident that He equips the called.

A spiritual boldness is rising in you. The David anointing is stirring — a battle-ready confidence, a holy defiance against fear. You are learning that courage is not the absence of fear but the willingness to act in spite of it. You're stepping into obedience, leaning into identity, and allowing your spirit to awaken to the power that has been inside you all along.

You are not the same person you were a few weeks ago. Fear is shrinking. Courage is expanding. Obedience is growing. Identity is strengthening. Your spirit is waking up to the truth that giants were never meant to intimidate you — they were meant to reveal God's power through your faithfulness.

Next week, you will move into life after the giant falls. Killing fear is powerful, but living fearlessly is transformational. Step forward with the tools, courage, and authority God has already placed in your hands. Your victory is not just coming — it is already unfolding.

Weekly Prayer

Dear Father,

Thank You for awakening the warrior inside me.

Thank You for training me, equipping me, and preparing me for victory.

Give me boldness to run toward the battles You've assigned to me.

Help me lay down what doesn't fit and use what You've placed in my hands.

Let courage rise and fear fall.

In Jesus' name,
Amen.

Week Five

Day 1: Warriors Don't Live Led by Emotion

Fear thrives when emotion leads. Panic spikes. Doubt rises. Feelings swirl. And suddenly, your decisions start aligning with anxiety instead of your identity. Fear's goal is simple: to make you react. Not think. Not pray. Not discern. Just react. Its aim is to hijack your mind, your choices, and your future by keeping you caught in the emotional storm.

But warriors don't live by emotional reaction. Warriors live by spiritual conviction. David didn't step onto the battlefield because he "felt brave." He stepped onto the battlefield because he was anchored. Anchored in who God was, who he was, and the covenant he carried. Courage isn't a fleeting feeling—it's a decision. Feelings fluctuate. Conviction anchors. Emotions lie. Identity stabilizes. When fear tries to hijack your emotions, it's attempting to hijack your destiny.

Fear wants your heart to dictate your actions. It wants your mood to determine your obedience. But a fearless warrior interrupts the emotional spiral and returns to truth. You pause and ask: "What did God say? What is actually true? What is fear trying to make me believe? What is the Holy Spirit whispering instead?" This is spiritual maturity: choosing obedience over emotion, trust over turmoil, and truth over anxiety.

It doesn't mean you won't feel afraid. Fear will still rise. Doubt will still whisper. But fear loses its vote when your decisions flow from identity rather than feelings. When your heart is anchored in the truth of who God says you are, your spirit stands firm even when circumstances shake. Your mind aligns with covenant promises rather than panic. Your choices reflect conviction rather than confusion.

Today, you stop letting your emotions drive your destiny. You stop letting fear dictate your responses. You anchor your heart in God's truth, in your identity, and in His calling. Every time fear tries to pull you off course, you remember: stability comes from spiritual conviction, not emotional reaction. You step into the day as a fearless warrior—grounded, disciplined, and ready to fight well, without retreating.

Bible Reading

READ EPH 6:10 (KJV)

Journal Prompt:

How often do emotions lead your decisions?

Choose one decision today and make it from conviction, not emotion.

A warrior who doesn't understand the enemy's tactics is always vulnerable. But a warrior who understands her enemy becomes dangerous. Awareness is your advantage. Fear uses the same predictable tactics over and over: distraction, delay, doubt, discouragement, and distortion. These are its tools. Its weapons. Its way of keeping you from stepping fully into who God called you to be.

Fear distracts you with noise. It fills your mind with chaos so you can't hear God's voice. Fear delays your obedience with overthinking, convincing you that waiting is safer than moving. Fear injects doubt into your thoughts, whispering lies about your capability, your calling, or your destiny. Fear discourages you with comparison, making you believe others are better equipped, smarter, or more favored. Fear distorts truth until you begin to question everything God has spoken to your heart. Sound familiar? Good. Because awareness is the enemy of fear.

The more you recognize fear's patterns, the faster you can dismantle them. Fear is not creative; it is repetitive. It relies on tactics that have worked in the past, targeting the areas where you are most vulnerable. But repetition is its weakness. Once you know the strategy, once you see the pattern, fear loses its element of surprise. You are no longer caught off guard. You no longer react unconsciously. You respond intentionally.

This is why Scripture commands, "Do not be ignorant of the enemy's schemes." Awareness is your armor. Knowledge is your weapon. When a warrior understands the enemy's methods, she can anticipate, resist, and overcome. She knows exactly what fear is trying to do and refuses to give it power. She shuts down its lies before they gain traction, interrupts its narratives before they take hold, and walks forward with confidence that God's authority is greater than any tactic fear can employ.

Today, study the battlefield to win the war. Pay attention to the patterns, the whispers, the delays, the doubts, and the distortions. Label them for what they are. Recognize them. Name them. And then move forward. Fear is predictable, but a prepared warrior is unstoppable. When you know your enemy, you are no longer a victim—you are a victor.

Bible Reading

READ EPH 6:11 (KJV)

Journal Prompt:

What tactic does fear use against you most?

Today's Challenge

Identify the top tactic fear uses on you — and interrupt it today.

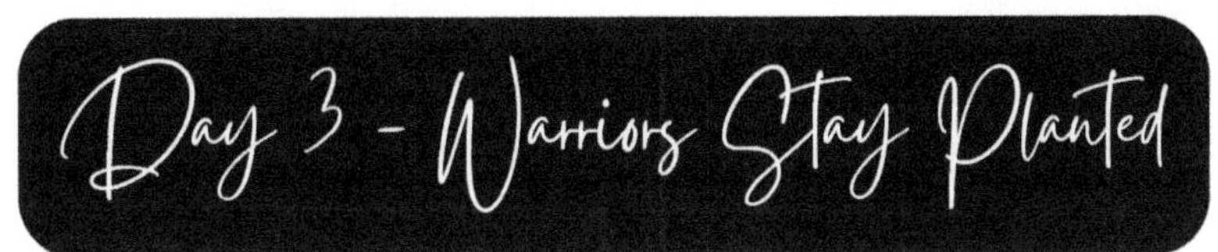

Fear thrives in instability. When your spiritual footing is loose, fear knocks you off balance with the slightest pressure. It preys on uncertainty, magnifies distraction, and whispers that the ground beneath you is shifting. This is why warriors learn to remain planted—rooted firmly in truth, identity, calling, God's presence, and spiritual discipline.

"Planted" doesn't mean rigid or inflexible. It means rooted. Deep, steady, unshakable. It means that no matter what storms rise, no matter what voices shout, no matter what fear tries to convince you, you stand firm because your foundation is in God. Warriors who stay rooted can withstand pressures that would destroy others. They don't collapse under comparison, criticism, or chaos. They don't sway with emotions, trends, or the expectations of others. They are anchored.

David is the ultimate example. He wasn't shaken by Goliath's size, noise, arrogance, or experience. Why? Because he wasn't rooted in the circumstances—he was rooted in God. His identity, courage, and confidence came from who God said he was, not from what he saw around him. Fear tries to uproot you emotionally, spiritually, and mentally. It wants you shifting—back and forth, in and out, yes and no, hesitant and doubtful. But warriors refuse to be moved by the shifting winds of fear. They stand firm on the ground God gave them.

Fear says mobility is safety. God says stability is strength. The rooted warrior knows this. Roots determine resilience. Roots feed courage. Roots feed endurance. Roots feed clarity. You cannot outrun fear, outthink fear, or outmaneuver fear if your foundation is weak. But when you are planted, fear loses its power to control you, to distract you, or to dictate your next step.

Today, evaluate your roots. Are you anchored in God's truth, in His promises, in your identity and calling? Or are you swaying with every emotion, thought, and circumstance? Plant yourself. Stand firm. Let your spiritual roots grow deep and wide. The storms will come, the giants will roar, the enemy will try to shake you—but you will not move. You will endure. You will stand. You will rise because stability is strength, and God is your foundation.

Bible Reading

READ EPH 6:14 (KJV)

Journal Prompt:

Where have you been spiritually unstable?

Commit to one spiritual routine this week (prayer, worship, Scripture) and stay rooted in it.

Even David had mighty men. Even Moses had Aaron and Hur. Even Paul had Timothy, Barnabas, Silas, Priscilla, and Aquila. Even Jesus had the disciples. Each of these leaders knew that the battle was never meant to be fought in isolation. Yet fear constantly whispers the opposite. Fear tries to convince you that isolation is safer, that handling life alone is stronger. Fear says, "Don't burden anyone," "No one will understand," "They'll think you're weak," "You're better off managing this by yourself."

But warriors understand a deeper truth: isolation makes you vulnerable, and community makes you unstoppable. The enemy attacks hardest where you stand alone. Fear grows fastest in the dark, feeding on secrecy, silence, and solitude. When you bring fear into the light—to God, to trusted sisters, to spiritual mentors—its power begins to break.

Warriors fight together. They lift one another's arms when fatigue sets in. They speak truth when someone forgets who she is. They pray when someone is weary. They stand guard when someone faces attack. Strength multiplies in community. Courage spreads when women stand shoulder to shoulder. Fear loses its grip when accountability, support, and shared faith enter the room.

God never intended for you to carry every battle alone. He places you in circles, teams, communities, and sisterhoods because He knows you are stronger together. This is why the Sisterhood and Mission Driven Church exist—to cultivate women who fight alongside one another, not against themselves. It's in this community that courage is reinforced, faith is sharpened, and obedience is encouraged.

Today, ask yourself: where are you trying to fight alone? Who can you bring into your battle—someone to pray with you, speak truth over you, or simply stand in solidarity? God designed connection as a strategic advantage, not a luxury. When you embrace the power of community, fear loses its stronghold. You no longer have to face the giants by yourself. Together, warriors rise. Together, fear is diminished. Together, the battle becomes a victory.

You are not meant to walk this path in isolation. You are meant to fight in community, supported, strengthened, and emboldened. Stand with your sisters. Lift each other. Fight together. Fear may still try to isolate you, but in unity, you are unstoppable.

Bible Reading

Journal Prompt:

Where have you been trying to fight alone?

Today's Challenge

Share one area of fear with someone safe — a mentor, leader, or trusted friend.

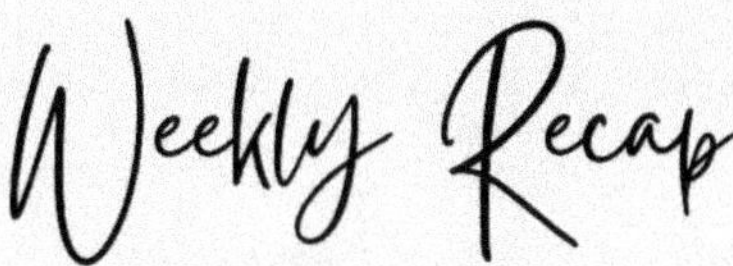

Weekly Recap

This week was about becoming unshakeable — the kind of woman the enemy fears. You discovered what it means to stand firm, anchored, and steady, even when fear tries to steal your peace. You learned that warriors don't let emotions lead, recognize the enemy's strategy, stay planted and rooted, and refuse to fight alone.

Fear wants you fragile. God is making you fortified. Fear wants you isolated. God is making you supported. Fear wants you emotional. God is making you anchored. Fear wants you confused. God is making you discerning.

You are not becoming a woman who avoids fear. You are becoming a woman who faces it head-on and refuses to retreat. This week strengthened your spirit, steadied your heart, stretched your discernment, and deepened your identity. You are learning to respond with clarity instead of reaction, conviction instead of hesitation, stability instead of chaos, and support instead of isolation.

A warrior is rising in you — a woman who refuses to back down, who stands firm in the face of opposition, who trusts in God's preparation and the community He places around her. You are learning that true strength is not just physical or emotional — it is spiritual, rooted in identity, fortified by obedience, and reinforced by connection.

Next week, you will confront one of fear's deepest strongholds: the agreements you've unknowingly made with fear that have shaped your life. That week is about deliverance, breakthrough, and spiritual turning points. It's about taking authority over the areas fear has crept into and reclaiming the ground God has already given you.

You are becoming unshakeable. Not because life is easier. Not because fear has disappeared. But because God is transforming your spirit, equipping you with power, wisdom, and courage to stand, fight, and win.

Weekly Prayer

Dear Father,

Thank You for strengthening me this week.

Thank You for building resilience, clarity, conviction, and community around me.

Help me walk as a fearless warrior — stable, supported, bold, and obedient.

Continue to steady my heart and sharpen my spirit as I rise into the woman You created me to be.

In Jesus' name,
Amen.

Week Six

Day 1: Agreements Give Fear Access

Fear isn't powerful on its own. It only gains power when you agree with it. A fearful thought comes, and you accept it. A lie whispers, and you believe it. A scenario flashes, and you rehearse it. A fear rises, and you obey it. Agreement is spiritual permission. Fear cannot dominate your life unless you say "yes" to its voice. Statements like "I'll always be anxious," "That's just who I am," "I can't handle this," or "People always leave" are not just thoughts — they are covenants, declarations written in the spiritual realm. Every agreement gives fear a foothold in your mind, your heart, and your choices.

Here's the good news: if you made an agreement, you can break it. Immediately. Completely. Permanently. Fear doesn't need permission to attack, but it needs permission to remain. Every agreement becomes a barrier to your calling, and every broken agreement becomes a doorway to freedom.

Awareness is the first step. Recognizing where fear has been speaking through you is the starting point for reclaiming authority over your mind, your decisions, and your life. You're beginning to see where fear has influenced your choices, shaped your reactions, and limited your obedience. You're beginning to see where God is calling you to speak back — to revoke permission, take authority, and declare freedom.

You don't have to wait for fear to leave, and you don't have to negotiate. You have the power to end every agreement that has kept fear in place. The moment you do, you step into the life God intended — fearless, free, fully alive, and fully His.

Bible Reading

READ PROVERBS 18:21 (KJV)

Journal Prompt:

What fearful statements have you repeated
about yourself?

Today's Challenge

Write one agreement with fear you've made.
Then cross it out and write God's truth.

Day 2 – Fear Uses Your Voice To Strengthen Its Grip

Fear doesn't just whisper — it wants you to repeat it. Your voice is powerful. Your words shape the atmosphere around you, the spiritual climate within you, and the direction of your future. Fear wants access to your voice because it knows this truth: whatever you speak grows. Fear grows when it's spoken. Faith grows when it's spoken. Every declaration you make feeds one kingdom or the other. When you say, "I'm overwhelmed," your body agrees. When you say, "This is impossible," your spirit agrees. When you say, "I can't do this," your courage agrees. These aren't harmless statements; they are agreements that carry spiritual weight. This isn't about positive thinking or motivational language — this is spiritual law. Heaven responds to faith. Hell responds to fear. Your words reveal which kingdom you're partnering with.

Fear wants to borrow your voice so it can strengthen its grip. It wants you to speak its lies until they feel like truth. It wants you to reinforce the very thing that's been attacking you. But the moment you begin speaking truth instead of fear, everything shifts. When you speak God's Word, you reinforce the Spirit within you instead of the fear coming against you. When you declare what God says, your identity strengthens. When you verbalize faith, courage begins to rise. Your voice is not neutral — it is a weapon. It can build prisons or break chains. It can strengthen fear or shatter it completely.

Today is about awareness. Where has fear borrowed your voice? Where have you repeated words that didn't come from God? Where have you spoken death over your peace, your future, your confidence, or your calling? You cannot always control the thoughts that show up, but you can control the words you release. And the moment you stop giving fear your voice is the moment fear starts losing its power. You are learning to partner your voice with truth, with faith, with identity, with heaven. Fear has spoken long enough. Today, you take your voice back.

Journal Prompt:

What fear-based sentences come out of your mouth most often?

God doesn't ask you to "manage" fear. He calls you to renounce it.

To renounce means to reject, to revoke, to break agreement with, to cancel legal right, to remove permission. Fear isn't emotional — it's legal. It uses your agreements as contracts. But the moment you renounce fear, the contract is void. Fear has no right. No claim. No authority. No power.

Renouncing fear sounds like: "I renounce the lie that I am unsafe." "I break agreement with fear of failure." "I reject fear of abandonment." "I revoke fear's influence over my decisions." "I cancel fear's legal right in my life."

This is spiritual warfare. Not dramatic. Not emotional. Just authoritative. Fear cannot withstand the authority of a daughter who breaks agreement. The enemy thrives on ignorance — but dies under authority.

Today, you are stepping into the courtroom of heaven and revoking every contract you never meant to sign. Every fear you've repeated, every lie you've agreed with, every scenario you've rehearsed — it no longer has permission to control your life. You are exercising the authority God gave you, and fear must bow.

Your voice, your declaration, your faith — these are the tools of renunciation. The moment you speak against fear with authority, its grip weakens. The agreements that once strengthened it are canceled. You are free to walk forward with boldness, confidence, and obedience.

Renouncing fear is not a suggestion. It's a spiritual position. It's a claim of freedom. And today, that freedom is yours.

Bible Reading

READ JAMES 4:7 (KJV)

Journal Prompt:

What agreements with fear do you now see clearly?

Today's Challenge

Write your top three agreements with fear.
Renounce each one out loud.

Breaking agreements is powerful — but it is only half the process.

After you break fear's agreements, you must replace them. Nature hates a vacuum. So does the spirit realm. If you break an agreement but fail to establish truth in its place, fear will return with a new strategy. Not because you're weak — but because unfilled space always gets filled.

Truth must replace every lie. Identity must replace every insecurity. Promise must replace every false future. Scripture must replace every accusation. God's truth is not just comfort — it is architecture. It builds something new inside you.

Where fear said, "You're alone," truth says, "God is with me." Where fear said, "You're unprepared," truth says, "I am equipped." Where fear said, "You're fragile," truth says, "I am strong in the Lord." Where fear said, "You're unsafe," truth says, "I am protected."

Replacing fear isn't about repeating affirmations — it's about establishing new agreements. Every truth you declare becomes a spiritual contract. Every promise you claim becomes a shield. Every identity you embrace becomes a foundation.

When truth becomes your new contract, fear loses its voice permanently. It can no longer occupy space that belongs to God's authority, promises, and power. The lies that once dictated your reactions are replaced with unshakable reality.

Today, identify every place fear has been speaking through you. Then speak God's truth into each one. Replace doubt with faith, insecurity with identity, and lies with Scripture. You are not just canceling fear — you are building a new spiritual structure in your life.

Fear will try to whisper again, but it has nowhere to land. Every agreement you break and every truth you establish is a victory. This is how freedom is cemented. This is how courage is anchored. This is how a fearless warrior is made.

Bible Reading

READ JOHN 17:17 (KJV)

Journal Prompt:

What truths do you need to establish today?

Today's Challenge

Write three new agreements with God's truth.
Declare them aloud.

Weekly Recap

This week was deliverance. Quiet, steady, deep deliverance.

You learned that fear:

◆ Gains power through agreement

◆ Uses your voice to reinforce those agreements

◆ Loses power the moment you renounce them

◆ Must be replaced with truth

This is one of the most important weeks in the entire series. Because agreements shape everything: your emotions, your identity, your reactions, your expectations, your decisions.

When you break agreements with fear, your entire internal structure changes. You stop thinking like the fearful version of yourself. You stop reacting like her.
You stop choosing like her. You stop living like her.

You begin stepping into identity. Authority. Confidence. Courage.

Fear doesn't need to be fought anymore — it needs to be replaced. This week, you tore down the contracts fear built.

Next week, you'll step into fearless relationships and decisions — areas where fear has quietly dictated your entire life story. Freedom is here. And it's only getting deeper.

Weekly Prayer

Dear Father,

Thank You for breaking every agreement I made with fear — knowingly or unknowingly.

Thank You for revealing truth, restoring identity, and reshaping my heart.

Help me stand firm in freedom.

Seal every new agreement with Your Spirit.

Teach me to walk boldly, confidently, and courageously into my next season.

In Jesus' name,
Amen.

Week Seven

Day 1: Fear Has Been Making Your Decisions

Fear doesn't just affect your emotions — it affects your choices.

Think about it: how many "no's" were actually fear? How many "yes's" were actually fear? How many detours were actually fear? How many delays were fear? How many relationships were fear? How many endings were fear? How many opportunities were fear? Fear has shaped more of your story than you realize.

Fear makes you choose safety over calling. Fear makes you choose comfort over growth. Fear makes you choose predictability over obedience. Fear makes you choose emotionally avoidant relationships over healthy ones. Fear makes you choose isolation over vulnerability.

Fear-based decisions feel wise, but they build a small, limited, suffocating life. They always sound like: "I don't want to get hurt." "I don't want to regret this." "I don't want to fail." "I don't want to be embarrassed." "I don't want to be disappointed again."

Fear-based decision-making is survival. Faith-based decision-making is destiny. When God leads you, He leads you through identity — not insecurity. When fear leads you, it leads you through self-protection — not purpose.

Fear is not allowed to be your decision-maker anymore. Today, God is inviting you to examine how fear has been directing your path — and reclaim that authority.

READ PROVERBS 3:6 (KJV)

Journal Prompt:

What major decisions in your life were shaped by fear?

Today's Challenge

Write one decision you've been delaying.
Ask God directly:
"What do You want me to do?"

Day 2 - Fear Distorts How You See Yourself

Fear doesn't just affect your decisions — it deeply affects your relationships.

Fear says: "You're too much." "You're not enough." "You're hard to love." "You're easily replaceable." "You have to earn your worth." "You should shrink to be accepted." "You should hide to stay safe."

And then those lies shape how you show up. Fear makes you over-give, over-attach, over-apologize, over-explain, over-function, over-please, over-guard. Fear convinces you to shrink your voice, silence your needs, and soften your boundaries. Fear forms relationships built on appeasement — not authenticity, on performance — not partnership, on fear of abandonment — not covenant love.

But God never designed relationships to be managed through fear. Relationships built on fear always break where they were never meant to bend.

Today, God is confronting the way fear has distorted how you see yourself — because your relationships cannot heal until your identity does. You were never meant to manage connections from fear. You were meant to show up as the daughter God created — whole, confident, worthy, and loved.

Journal Prompt:

How has fear shaped how you show up in relationships?

Today's Challenge

Write three identity statements God says about you —
and one relational fear they replace.

A woman who lives in fear cannot have healthy boundaries. Her boundaries will always be too loose (to avoid conflict) or too rigid (to avoid vulnerability).

Fear-based boundaries sound like: "I don't want to upset anyone." "I don't want them to leave." "I don't want to be taken advantage of." "I don't want to need anyone." "I don't want to depend on anyone." Fear either makes you let people too close too quickly or not close enough at all.

Boundaries rooted in fear protect your wounds, not your worth. Boundaries rooted in God protect your identity, your peace, your calling, your emotional health, your spiritual growth.

Healthy boundaries require courage — courage to tell the truth, courage to disappoint people, courage to say no, courage to choose yourself, courage to protect what God placed inside you. Fear has no place in your boundaries anymore.

Today, God is teaching you how to protect yourself through wisdom, not fear.

READ PROVERBS 4:23 (KJV)

Journal Prompt:

Where have you had fear-based boundaries?

Today's Challenge

Choose one relationship and write one boundary you need to strengthen.

Fear has influenced enough of your decisions. It does not get to influence your future.

Fear has told you to stay small. Fear has told you to stay safe. Fear has told you not to try. Fear has told you not to dream. Fear has told you to avoid risk. Fear has told you to expect disappointment. Fear has told you to lower your standards.

Fear has told you to assume the worst, and prepare for disaster, and anticipate rejection, and expect heartbreak.

But God is calling you into a future fear cannot shape. A future defined by identity, purpose, obedience, calling, clarity, courage, and faith.

Your future will not be written by fear. Your decisions will not be filtered through insecurity. Your relationships will not be shaped by self-protection. You will not be a woman influenced by fear — you will be a woman influenced by God.

Today is the day you stop letting fear have the final say. Your next yes, your next decision, your next relationship, your next step, your next season, your next calling — all of it belongs to God now, not fear.

Bible Reading

READ 2 TIM 1:7 (KJV)

Journal Prompt:
What future decisions have fear been shaping?

Write one major future-oriented decision you want fear removed from —
and surrender it to God.

Weekly Recap

This week, God confronted the areas where fear has shaped your story the most: your connections, your boundaries, your decisions, your future.

You discovered that fear has been making many of your decisions. Fear has distorted how you see yourself in relationships. Fear has created unhealthy boundaries. Fear has shaped your future thinking.

But now, you're stepping into a new way of living. A fearless woman shows up authentically, loves without shrinking, creates healthy boundaries, makes decisions from identity, discerns instead of panics, trusts instead of fears, and moves forward instead of retreating.

God is rewriting your inner world. He is restoring the places fear once dictated. He is healing the parts of you that made fear feel reasonable. He is strengthening your voice, your identity, and your capacity to connect.

Next week is your final week — and it's all about stepping into a fearless future and staying free.

Weekly Prayer

Dear Father,

Thank You for healing my relationships, decisions, and identity this week.

Thank You for showing me where fear influenced my choices and for giving me courage to choose differently.

Lead me into a future shaped by You alone.

Help me love boldly, choose wisely, and walk courageously.

In Jesus' name,
Amen.

Week Eight

Fear didn't just attack your emotions. It attacked your identity. For years, fear tried to tell you who you were: fragile, insecure, unqualified, unlovable, unsafe, inadequate, not ready, not enough.

Fear tried to shape the story you told yourself. Fear tried to write your future before you even lived it. Fear tried to limit what you believed you could become.

But here's the truth: fear lied. Every. Single. Time. You are not who fear said you were. You are who God says you are.

And God says you are: chosen, strong, capable, protected, called, anointed, courageous, victorious, deeply loved, spiritually powerful.

Fear built an identity around your worst moments — God builds your identity around your destiny. Fear magnified your weaknesses — God magnifies your purpose. Fear rehearsed your failures — God reveals your calling. Fear assumed your pain was permanent — God has been writing redemption all along.

This is the week where you finally release the fearful version of yourself and embrace the woman you have become. You are no longer defined by fear. You are defined by God.

READ EPHESIANS 2:10 (KJV)

Journal Prompt:

What identities did fear try to put on you?

Write a letter to the "fearful version" of yourself —
and release her.

Fear taught you how to survive. God is teaching you how to live. Fear taught you to avoid risk. God teaches you to walk in faith. Fear taught you to react. God teaches you to discern. Fear taught you to protect yourself at all costs. God teaches you to trust His protection. Fear taught you to shrink. God teaches you to rise.

Fear led you into survival mode — always calculating, always preparing for the worst, always anticipating pain, always trying to control outcomes. Survival mode feels responsible... but it is actually fear in disguise.

Courage is not reckless. Courage is obedience. Courage doesn't mean you feel brave — it means you move even when you feel afraid.

This is the transition week: the week you stop living from past trauma and start living from present victory. The week you stop anticipating loss and start anticipating God. The week you stop letting fear manage your life and start letting courage lead it.

Survival is what happens when fear leads. Freedom is what happens when God leads.

Bible Reading

Journal Prompt:

Where has survival mode shaped your life?

Today's Challenge

Write one courageous step God is calling you into —
and commit to taking it.

Fear is territorial.
It doesn't want to leave easily.
Even after you break agreements,
fear often tries to follow.

It whispers familiar lies.
It attempts old patterns.
It knocks on the same emotional doors.
It tries to re-enter through old wounds.

But this time, everything is different.

Why?
Because YOU are different.

You are not the version of yourself fear used to control.
You are not living from the same beliefs.
You are not operating from the same identity.
You are not carrying the same agreements.
You are not navigating life with the same insecurity.

Fear may knock —
but you no longer open the door.

Fear may whisper —
but you no longer repeat it.

Fear may trigger old feelings —
but you no longer live under them.

Fear cannot rule a woman who knows who she is.

Fear follows you into your future only if you allow it.
This week, you revoke its invitation.

Your future is not fear-shaped.
Your future is God-shaped.

READ PSALM 34:4 (KJV)

Journal Prompt:

How has fear tried to follow you into new seasons?

Today's Challenge

Identify one fear that tries to return.
Declare:
"You are not coming with me."

This is your commissioning moment. You are not finishing a study — you are stepping into a new identity. You are not wrapping up eight weeks — you are beginning a new way of living. You are not just learning about fear — you have dethroned it.

Every truth you've learned, every agreement you've broken, every identity you've embraced, every battle you've fought, every giant you've faced, every step of courage you've taken — has been leading to THIS moment.

The moment where fear is no longer your master. The moment where courage becomes your default. The moment where obedience becomes your normal. The moment where freedom becomes your foundation.

God is commissioning you into fearless faith, fearless purpose, fearless relationships, fearless obedience, fearless calling, fearless identity, fearless decisions, and a fearless future.

This is not a temporary transformation. This is spiritual reformation. Fear had its chapter — but it does not get to write your book.

This final day is not an ending — it's an activation.

Bible Reading

READ ISAIAH 60:1 (KJV)

Journal Prompt:
What has God transformed most in you?

Weekly Recap

This is not the end of a study. This is the beginning of a new life.

You have dismantled fear at every level: emotional, mental, relational, spiritual, decisional, generational.

You have become a woman fear can no longer intimidate. A woman who runs toward giants. A woman who stands firm. A woman who discerns. A woman who lives rooted. A woman who hears God clearly. A woman who obeys courageously. A woman who moves boldly.

Fear once shaped your identity — now identity shapes your courage. Fear once made your decisions — now discernment leads your steps. Fear once controlled your imagination — now faith fuels your future.

This final week has been a commissioning — a divine activation into who you were always meant to be. The future ahead of you is not fear-managed. It is Spirit-led. It is God-designed. It is courage-fueled. It is destiny-marked.

This is who you are now: a fearless, faith-filled, obedient daughter of God who knows her identity, walks in authority, and refuses to bow to fear ever again.

Weekly Prayer

Dear Father,

Thank You for transforming me from the inside out.

Thank You for breaking fear, restoring identity, renewing my mind, and commissioning me into a fearless life.

Seal this freedom deeply within me.

Lead me into my calling with clarity and confidence.

I will walk boldly, courageously, and obediently into every place You send me.

In Jesus' name,
Amen.

If you've made it to the end of this journey, hear me clearly: you are a different woman now. Fear may still whisper, but it no longer rules. Fear may still show up, but it no longer leads. Fear may still knock, but you no longer open the door.

You are stronger. You are braver. You are clearer. You are spiritually awake in a way fear cannot undo. You did hard things these eight weeks. You confronted lies. You faced giants. You chose truth when fear screamed louder. You stepped into the identity God placed inside you before you were born.

And this is just the beginning. My prayer is that you step forward with a new confidence — not the confidence that says, "I'm not afraid," but the confidence that says, "Even if fear shows up, I move anyway." **Courage isn't the absence of fear.** *It's the refusal to bow to it.*

You are not a woman waiting for permission. You are a woman commissioned by God. So go. Say yes. Step forward. Pick up your stone. Run toward your giant. Your life is bigger than your fear. Your calling is louder than your insecurity. Your God is greater than anything standing in front of you.

Walk boldly, Sis. You were never called to be afraid.

If this study stirred something in you...
If you're craving connection...
If you're ready to build real relationships...

I want to personally invite you into two communities built exactly for that:

Mission Driven Sisters: A global sisterhood for women who want authentic friendship, support, growth, and faith-filled conversations. Join us at MissionDrivenSisters.com.

Mission Driven Church: An online group of believers focused on living out their faith — including small groups, prayer, teaching, and a family that actually walks life with you. Visit us at MissionDrivenChurch.com to learn more.

You don't have to pretend.
You don't have to isolate to feel safe.
You don't have to be strong alone.

There is a place for you — a real one.

And it's waiting.

I am so proud of you.

With love, strength, and sisterhood,

Continue Your Journey Toward Freedom

What you've just worked through is only one part of a bigger story.

The *You Are Not Called* series was created to help Christian women break free from the emotional struggles that quietly keep them stuck—often beneath the surface of faith, responsibility, and strength.

Each book in the series focuses on a different area where many women feel trapped, overwhelmed, or disconnected, including anger, anxiety, loneliness, fear, and shame.

While each study can be read on its own, the greatest transformation often happens when these truths are layered together over time.

If this book resonated with you, you're not alone—and you don't have to stop here.

The *You Are Not Called* Series
Continue your journey with the other studies in the series:

You Are Not Called to Be Angry
A Bible Study for Christian Women Ready to Break Free from Anger

You Are Not Called to Be Anxious
A Bible Study for Christian Women Ready to Break Free from Anxiety

You Are Not Called to Be Alone
A Bible Study for Christian Women Ready to Break Free from Loneliness

You Are Not Called to Be Afraid
A Bible Study for Christian Women Ready to Break Free from Fear

You Are Not Called to Be Ashamed
A Bible Study for Christian Women Ready to Break Free from Shame

Each book builds on the biblical truth about who you are and your calling — helping you heal deeply, renew your mind, and walk forward in the freedom God has always intended for you.

A Final Word Before You Go

You don't have to rush this process. Healing is not a race—it's a relationship.

As you continue through the series, allow God to meet you where you are, speak truth into the places that feel tender, and gently lead you forward. You are not behind. You are not broken. And you are not alone on this journey.

God has more for you—and freedom is closer than you think.

Free Resources

Hey there, superstar!

You've made it through the book, and I'm so proud of you. But let's be real - reading is just the first step. Now it's time to put all this good stuff into practice. And because I'm not about to send you out there empty-handed, I've got some awesome resources to help you on your journey.

Think of these as your anger management toolkit. They're like the Swiss Army knife of emotional growth - versatile, handy, and they might just save you in a pinch (though maybe don't try to use them to open a can or cut down a small tree).

To access the resources, simply create your free account at www.youarenotcalled.com.

Inside, you'll have to the above resources plus much more!